GRAMERCY GREAT MASTERS

PG MS

Acknowledgments

The publishers would like to thank the museums for reproduction permission and in particular the **BRIDGEMAN ART LIBRARY** and **SCALA Istituto Fotografico Editoriale** for their help in supplying the illustrations for the book.

Board of Trustees of the V&A: The Miraculous Draft of Fishes.

Galleria Borghese, Rome: Madonna and Child with the Infant St. John the Baptist ("The Madonna of the Goldfinch").

Galleria degli Uffizi, Florence: Pope Leo X with Cardinals Giulio de' Medici and Luigi de' Rossi; Portrait of a Young Man, probably Francesco Maria della Rovere, Duke of Urbino; Self-Portrait.

Galleria dell'Accademia, Florence: The Entombment.

Hermitage, St. Petersburg: The Madonna of the Book ("The Connestabile Madonna").

Louvre, Paris: St. Michael and the Devil; Portrait of Baldassare Castiglione; St. George and the Dragon; The Holy Family ("Madonna of Francis I").

Museum of Fine Arts, Budapest: The Madonna and the Child with the Infant St. John the Baptist ("The Esterhezy Madonna").

National Gallery, London: The Madonna and Child with the Infant St. John the Baptist ("The Aldobrandini Madonna"); The Madonna and Child with the Infant St. John the Baptist ("La Belle Jardinière"); The Madonna and Child with St. John the Baptist and St. Nicholas of Bari ("The Ansidei Madonna").

National Gallery of Scotland, Edinburgh: The Bridgewater Madonna.

Palazzo della Farnesina, Rome: The Triumph of Galatea.

Palazzo Pitti, Florence: Portrait of Agnolo Doni; Madonna and Child ("Madonna del Granduca"); Portrait of a Lady with a Veil ("La Donna Velata"); The Madonna of the Chair ("Madonna della Sedia"); The Madonna Enthroned with Four Saints ("The Madonna of the Baldacchino"); Portrait of Maddalena Doni.

Pinacoteca Comunale, Città di Castello: The Trinity with St. Sebastian and St. Roch.

Pinacoteca di Brera, Milan: The Marriage of the Virgin.

Prado Museum, Madrid: The Holy Family with the Infant St. John the Baptist ("The Madonna of the Rose"); The Way to Calvary ("Lo Spasimo"); The Holy Family with a Lamb.

Pushkin Museum, Moscow: Madonna and Child with Beardless St. Joseph.

Staatliche Kunstsammlungen, Dresden: The Sistine Madonna.

Stanze di Raffaello, Vaticano, Rome: The Coronation of Charlemagne.

Vatican Library, Rome: The Fire in the Borgo.

Vatican Museum and Galleries, Rome: The Transfiguration; God Creating Animals; Pope Leo I Repulsing Attila; The Liberation of St. Peter; The Expulsion of Heliodorus from the Temple; The Mass of Bolsena; The Wall of the Stanza della Segnatura illustrating Jurisprudence; Parnassus; The Disputation over the Sacrament ("The Disputa"); The School of Athens.

Published by Gramercy Books
distributed by Random House Value Publishing, Inc.
40 Engelhard Avenue
Avenel, New Jersey 07001

Printed and bound in Italy

ISBN: 0-517-12401-7

10 9 8 7 6 5 4 3 2 1

Raphael

GRAMERCY BOOKS

NEW YORK • AVENEL

Raphael
His Life and Works

The Italian Renaissance began in the second half of the 1300s and spanned some two hundred and fifty years. The cultural life of the country flourished in this period, which takes its name from a word meaning "rebirth," and there was a vigorous revival of painting, sculpture, architecture and classical studies after an interval of many centuries.

In art, the religious and philosophical themes of the Renaissance were treated with a new sense of freedom and experimentation. Renaissance art sought to understand the real nature of the subject portrayed rather than provide a slavish reproduction. The recently developed technique of perspective used a geometrical technique to represent three-dimensional space, and figures and objects could at last be convincingly placed in a picture, allowing the onlooker to establish closer contact with the scene.

Renaissance nobles patronized the arts, using them not only to embellish their sumptuous courts but also as tangible demonstrations of their power. The city-states of Italy became bustling cultural centers, thronged with scholars, humanists, artists and craftsmen.

Duke Federico II da Montefeltro established his refined and sophisticated court in the city of Urbino, which was remodeled by architects Luciano Laurana and Francesco di Giorgio Martini in keeping with the ideals of Renaissance rationalism. The Italian painters Piero della Francesca and Paolo Uccello came to work in the city, followed by foreigners such as the Fleming Justus of Ghent and Pedro Berruguete from Spain. Urbino was bathed in an atmosphere of learning and culture, and this was the milieu in which Raphael matured and received his earliest training.

FROM URBINO TO UMBRIA

Raphael was born Raffaello Sanzio in Urbino on April 6, 1483. He was the son of Giovanni Santi, from whom he took the name of Sanzio, which is derived from the Latinized form *Santius*. Giovanni was a minor painter who worked for the Montefeltro court, and he gave Raphael his first lessons in art in his own workshop. Here Raphael met Timoteo della Vite, a painter and dealer in pictures who had recently returned from an apprenticeship in Bologna. Giovanni soon noted his son's talent, and he asked della Vite to show Raphael a selection of pictures by both Italian and foreign artists. These pictures, which probably included works by Flemish painters, as well as some by Piero della Francesca and other artists well known at the court of Urbino, seem to have made a vivid impression on young Raphael, and they gave him a firm foundation on which he could later build.

Raphael's mother, Magia di Battista di Nicola Ciarla, died in 1491. The historian Giorgio Vasari, in his *Lives of the Most Eminent Painters, Sculptors and Architects*, which was published in 1550, declares that she nurtured a strong love for her only child, suckling him herself and bringing him up in the family home, a rare situation at the time for persons of this social standing. This tragic loss was followed three years later by the death of Giovanni Santi. At the age of eleven Raphael was an orphan.

It is generally believed that soon after his father's death Raphael began studying with Perugino in the Umbrian town of Perugia. His first known work, *The Blessed Nicola of Tolentino*, dates from 1500. The contract for this painting, which was done for the Church of Sant'Agostino at Città di Castello, explicitly stated that he was a "master" of his craft, and that he was helped by another artist, Evangelista da Pian di Meleto, who had worked with Raphael's father in Urbino. A violent earthquake in 1789 caused irreparable damage to the picture, and only two fragments have survived.

The distinct influence of Perugino can be seen in Raphael's early works. For example, Vasari declared that the *Mond Crucifixion*, painted in 1503 for another church at Città di Castello, could be mistaken for Perugino's work "if Raphael had not written his name." However, the openness of the landscape and the geometrical scheme of the painting recall the style of Urbino, and perhaps Raphael was looking back to Piero della Francesca's art, which had provided his teacher Perugino with much inspiration.

Raphael may have made a first visit to Rome in 1503 to see the enthronement of Pope Julius II, who was related to his patron and protectress, Giovanna Feltria della Rovere, Duchess of Sinigaglia. While in Rome, Raphael is believed to have met Pintoricchio, who at the time was designing the frescoes for the Piccolomini Library at the Cathedral of Siena, and he is said to have offered his help when it was time for them to be painted.

Another of Raphael's early works, from about 1503, is the diptych whose two panels are *The Knight's Dream* and *The Three Graces*. *The Knight's Dream*, which symbolizes Scipio, the Roman general who defeated Hannibal, choosing between the beauty of Venus and the strength and wisdom of Athena, is a fine example of compositional balance. The laurel tree at the center divides the panel in two; beneath it lies the sleeping knight and on each side stands a female figure. *The Three Graces* portrays the sequel to this episode, as the Hesperides offer the knight their golden apples as a reward for having chosen virtue.

Soon after returning to Umbria, Raphael completed his *Coronation of the Virgin* for the Oddi Chapel in the Church of San Francesco al Prato in Perugia. The winged cherub heads in the upper part of this picture seem to anticipate the *Disputa* fresco, completed several years later in the Stanza della Segnatura of the Vatican in Rome.

The *Marriage of the Virgin* was painted for the Church of San Francesco in Città di Castello. Signed "Raphael Urbinas" above the central arch of the portico of the temple, the date of 1504 can be read as "M" and "DIIII" on the pendentives. The painting was inspired by an altarpiece of the same subject started by Perugino for a chapel in the Cathedral of Perugia in 1500. Both compositions present a group of figures set before a vast square with a temple in the background, but in Raphael's version the foreground figures are arranged in a very natural manner, in contrast to Perugino's symmetrical and rigidly aligned figures.

Raphael's temple is much more harmoniously proportioned than Perugino's, and the higher viewpoint used by Raphael allows him to make better use of the perspective effect on the paving of the square. In this painting, Raphael has fully mastered the new principles of High Renaissance architecture, enabling him to leave behind the models provided by his former teacher and to concentrate on painting in the "modern manner."

RAPHAEL IN FLORENCE

When Raphael settled in Florence about 1504, the city was ruled by a handful of rich and powerful nobles, who sought to consolidate their control of the city with ambitious projects for paintings and sculptures. Leading artists were granted important public and private commissions, and their works were considered contributions to the enhanced prestige of Florence.

It was at this time that Leonardo da Vinci and Michelangelo returned to the city after long periods elsewhere. The fact that they were entrusted with the portrayal of the two most brilliant victories of the Florentine army is a significant indication of the fame they had achieved.

It was probably while he was working with Pintoricchio on the frescoes of the Piccolomini Library in Siena that Raphael heard of the change of artistic climate in Florence, and of the cartoons being prepared by Leonardo and Michelangelo for their enormous paintings of *The Battle of Anghiari* and *The Battle of Cascina* respectively, destined for the walls of the Council Chamber in the Palazzo della Signoria. Raphael promptly left Siena, and in Florence he was able to study virtually any painting that attracted his interest thanks to the influence of his patron Giovanna Feltria della Rovere. In a letter to Florence's chief magistrate Pier Soderini dated October 1, 1504, the perceptive duchess liberally praised the young artist from Urbino, declaring that "being greatly committed to his craft, he has decided to stay for some time in Florence to learn."

Raphael lost little time in absorbing these new lessons. He explored a range of contrasting techniques such as the *sfumato* effects and pyramidal compositions used by Leonardo and the dynamic tension developed by Michelangelo, without ignoring his own preferences for the "naturalness" of images and their

An Allegory
("Vision of a Knight")
(detail)

relation to the posture and emotional state of the figures portrayed.

Although Raphael adopted the basic elements of Leonardo's style of composition, he rejected the many symbolic implications and psychological overtones that were so dear to Leonardo. Raphael's new emphasis is especially evident in the portraits of Maddelena Doni and her husband Agnolo Doni from 1506. The three-quarter views of the sitters, who are set against spacious landscapes, echo the composition of Leonardo's *Mona Lisa* but achieve totally different expressive effects. Raphael precisely depicts the features, clothes, jewels and landscapes that form the backdrop for his patrons, while Leonardo invents a play of light and shade that masks the clarity of physical details and creates a sense of ambiguity and mystery with the eternally wistful smile of the *Mona Lisa*.

Traces of Leonardo's influence can also be seen in the pyramidal composition of several other works of Raphael's Florentine period, notably his *Belvedere Madonna*, *Belle Jardinière* and *Madonna of the Goldfinch*, all painted around 1506–1507.

From Michelangelo, Raphael learned how important it was to draw well. He also gained new insights into the dramatic potential of movement and the necessity of convincingly depicting reality by rendering volume. In the *Bridgewater Madonna* of 1507, for example, the strong sense of movement with which the Holy Child is endowed strongly recalls Michelangelo's *Taddei Tondo*. Michelangelo's influence can also be seen in *The Deposition*, commissioned by Atalanta Baglioni for her family's chapel in the Church of San Francesco al Prato in Perugia. Finished in 1507, the panel was intended to draw a parallel between the patron's grief for the murder of her son Grifonetto and the despair of Mary for her crucified child. The composition features two contrasting groups of figures. On the left, in the foreground, the body of Christ — closely resembling Michelangelo's *Pietà* — is being carried towards the tomb, while behind on the right is a group of women who have stopped to support the swooning Mary.

Raphael's period in Florence was interspersed with visits to Perugia and Urbino. He maintained cordial contacts with the

14

court of Urbino, and in 1505 he painted the diptych of *St. George and the Dragon* and *St. Michael and the Devil* for the Montefeltro family. The vigorous depiction of the horse and rider in the *St. George* confirms that Raphael had studied Leonardo's cartoons for the *Battle of Anghiari* with close attention, while the demonic images of the *St. Michael* suggest Flemish influences.

In 1508, Raphael made attempts to obtain a commission for a painting in the same room as the gigantic battle scenes of Michelangelo and Leonardo, but the commission was never awarded. Shortly after, while he was working on *The Madonna of the Baldacchino*, showing the Assembly of Saints gathered round the throne of the Virgin Mary against a grandiose architectural backdrop, he was summoned by Pope Julius II to participate in the decoration of the papal apartments in the Vatican. He abandoned the painting, and by January 1509 he was in Rome.

JULIUS II AND THE VATICAN STANZE

In 1309, Pope Clement V transferred the papal court from Rome to Avignon, and the papacy was dominated by the French until the court was brought back to Rome in 1377 by Gregory XI. A long series of popes then invested notable resources in a bid to restore Rome to its ancient splendor. In the first decades of the sixteenth century the Eternal City was graced by the noblest achievements of the High Renaissance, represented by the works of Bramante, Michelangelo and Raphael.

Two popes in particular, Julius II (1503–1513) and Leo X (1513–1521), shared a desire to endow the city with magnificent buildings and works of art. This was vital if the papacy was to recover its position as the principal center of religious and political power. Bramante, Michelangelo and Raphael were entrusted by Julius II with key works in this process of restoration.

The decoration of the famous Vatican Stanze, or papal apartments, had its origins in the refusal of Julius II to use the rooms occupied by his predecessor Alexander VI, with their frescoes by Pintoricchio, as his official residence. Initially, the only parts of the new apartments to be painted were the ceilings, to be done by artists from different regions, including Perugino, Sodoma, Baldassare Peruzzi, Bramantino and Lorenzo Lotto, joined by Raphael in 1509.

The Three Graces
(detail)

16

Julius II soon recognized that Raphael was remarkably adept at transforming the papal inspiration into reality, and he was invited to paint the frescoes of the Stanza della Segnatura, the room where official letters were signed. On the ceiling Raphael painted the personifications of *Theology*, *Philosophy*, *Jurisprudence* and *Poetry* set within circular enclosures above the lunettes of the walls. In the corners were *Astronomy*, *The Judgment of Solomon*, *The Sins of the Fathers* and *Apollo and Marsyas*. The original project was then amplified, and between 1509 and 1511 the walls were painted in the traditional manner of medieval and Renaissance libraries, with one wall each dedicated to Theology, Philosophy, Jurisprudence and Poetry.

The Stanza della Segnatura reflects the three fundamental elements of the human spirit as interpreted by the Neo-Platonic philosophy of the Renaissance: Truth, reached by the paths of Faith (*The Disputa* or *The Disputation Concerning the Blessed Sacrament*) and Science (*The School of Athens*); Good, achieved by the exercise of Justice (*Justice* and *Cardinal and Theological Virtues*); and Beauty, expressed by poetic creativity (*Parnassus*).

In these frescoes, Raphael involved the figures in scenes that allowed him to characterize them with different movements, expressions and postures. In *The Disputa* the Church Triumphant, shown by a group of heavenly saints, apostles and prophets set on a semicircle of clouds on either side of the Holy Trinity and St. John the Baptist, dominates the terrestrial realm of the Church Militant from above. The name of this fresco is derived from a mistaken interpretation of a passage by Giorgio Vasari, and the figures depicted are *discussing* rather than *disputing* the miraculous nature of the Blessed Sacrament. To emphasize the importance of this fundamental article of faith, Raphael places it at the convergence point of the perspective lines shown by the paving in the foreground. Many of the figures in the lower section have been identified: Bramante is leaning against the baluster to the left, Pope Sixtus IV is standing on the right, and behind him appears the head of Dante, crowned with laurel.

The School of Athens shows a building of majestic proportions, with a group of philosophers and sages gathered around Plato and Aristotle. These two figures represent the dual poles of

Renaissance thought, as Plato points up towards the world of ideas and Aristotle motions downwards to indicate the world of experience. As in *The Disputa*, several of the characters bear a marked resemblance to artists, humanists and other figures of the papal court. Euclid has been given the features of Bramante, Plato those of Leonardo, while Heraclitus has been recognized as Michelangelo, and Raphael and Sodoma can be seen in the extreme right of the lunette. A sign of the growing rivalry between Raphael and Michelangelo was the exclusion of the figure of Michelangelo as Heraclitus from the first cartoon prepared for this fresco. Only after the first part of Michelangelo's work in the Sistine Chapel had been unveiled and greatly admired was Raphael compelled by Julius II to insert his competitor's likeness.

In *Parnassus*, Raphael had to work around a window in the middle of the wall. The solution that he found follows an ascending and circular rhythm that moves up towards the center of the picture, showing poets of the ancient and modern worlds around Apollo and the Muses by the Castalian Spring.

The window of the fourth wall was not exactly at the center, and this suggested yet another possible arrangement to Raphael. He placed the Virtues at the top of the composition, and on either side of the window painted scenes representing civil and canon law, *Tribonianus Presenting the Pandects to the Emperor Justinian* and *Pope Gregory IX Approving the Decretals*.

In the summer of 1511, while he was still working in the Stanza della Segnatura, Raphael was already preparing to decorate a second room in the papal apartments, which was the Stanza d'Eliodoro, intended for audiences. It was a moment of great uncertainty for the Church of Rome. Julius II had convened the fifth Lateran Council, and the choice of the subjects for the new room was of particular religious and political significance. God was to be shown intervening to aid the Church, with clear references to the program of Julius, who had declared himself to be the "Liberator of the Faith."

On the two windowless walls are *The Expulsion of Heliodorus from the Temple* and *Pope Leo I Repulsing Attila*, while the other two walls are occupied by *The Mass of Bolsena* and *The Liberation of St. Peter*.

Lady with a Unicorn
(detail)

19

The first of the frescoes to be completed was *The Expulsion of Heliodorus*. On the right is Heliodorus, overwhelmed by the furious assault of the knight sent by God after he has been caught trying to steal the Temple treasure. Julius II watches from the left, symbolizing the victorious conflict to be waged against anyone who threatens the worldly riches of the Church. The handling of light in the scene imparts great dramatic intensity, with reflections that emphasize the perspective images of the arches, the domes of the nave, and the energetic figures.

The Mass of Bolsena alludes to Julius's devotion to the Eucharist, and contrasts the jostling crowd on the left with the aristocratic calm of the members of the papal retinue. The symmetry of the wall was impaired by a window, but Raphael exploited this shortcoming by placing the ceremonial altar above the window, at the center of the composition.

Pope Leo I Repulsing Attila represents an episode that took place in 452, when the advance of Attila and his invading army was halted by Leo and, as legend has it, by the appearance of an angel. Behind the Huns lies a trail of burning ruins, while above the pope and his attendants, moving forward to protect the Eternal City seen in the background, fly St. Peter and St. Paul, brandishing swords.

It is in *The Liberation of St. Peter* that Raphael uses his talent for illumination to the best advantage. The fresco is divided into three contiguous episodes. At the center is the glowing apparition of the Angel in the prison, where St. Peter lies in chains. On the right the Angel leads the saint to freedom, past two guards engulfed by an impenetrable and unnatural slumber. To the left the soldiers awaken to discover the escape of their prisoner, and the darkness of the night is lit by the moon and the flickering torch.

The Stanza d'Eliodoro, finished in 1514, shows how rapidly Raphael's art evolved to suit the tastes of the sixteenth century. The solemn calm of the Stanza della Segnatura has been superseded by intensely dramatic compositions full of movement and contrasts of light, foreshadowing in many ways the development of the Baroque School.

Portrait of a Woman
("La Muta")

The Alba Madonna
(detail)

PORTRAITS AND RELIGIOUS PAINTINGS

In the years between 1509 and 1514 Raphael worked at a frenzied pace. In addition to completing his frescoes in the Vatican Stanze he also turned out many portraits and altarpieces, mostly variations on the Madonna and Child theme.

In his portraits, Raphael repeated compositional schemes successfully used in previous years, paying great attention to the detailed depiction of the status and character of his sitters. For instance, in *Julius II* of 1512, Raphael's illustrious patron is seated and seen in a three-quarter view, his gaze directed downwards in meditation. The overall effect is that the viewer is actually standing beside the pope, as if there were no physical or spiritual separation between the sitter and ourselves.

An even more striking portrait is that of *Baldassare Castiglione* (1514–1515), a poet and scholar who was a member of many courts of Italy, Urbino included, before he moved to Rome. The portrait gives us the impression that the sitter is directly before us, and that we are able to share in his friendship with the artist. In *La Donna Velata* (1515–1516) Raphael creates a similar sense of intimacy, but lavishes greater attention on the depiction of the folds in the woman's dress.

In his altarpieces Raphael achieved the same direct contact with the spectator, revolutionizing schemes that had lasted for centuries. In the *Foligno Madonna* (1511–1512) John the Baptist looks straight out from the picture while he points towards the Virgin Mary. The influence of Leonardo's *Adoration of the Magi* is apparent, but the Holy Child seems to derive from Michelangelo's *Doni Tondo*. The panel was probably commissioned by Sigismondo de' Conti, seen kneeling on the right. It symbolizes his gratitude for the miraculous escape of his house at Foligno from damage by lightning, and this episode is shown in the background.

The *Sistine Madonna* was painted between 1513 and 1514 for the high altar of the church of the Benedictine Monastery in Piacenza. The Virgin Mary descends from heaven with the Holy Child on a canopy of clouds suffused with light, and these two figures look directly at the viewer. St. Sixtus seems to be pointing out a crowd of worshipers to the Virgin.

From the same period are *The Madonna of the Chair* and the *St. Cecily* altarpiece, commissioned for the Church of San Giovanni in Monte at Bologna. The subject is the ecstasy of St. Cecily; only she is able to hear the celestial harmonies symbolized by a choir of angels that appears among the clouds. The saints around her have all been given different postures: St. Paul is deep in meditation on the left, while on the right Mary Magdalene seems to invite the participation of the viewer with her penetrating gaze. In the background, St. John and St. Augustine exchange glances charged with significance. Here, Raphael has masterfully succeeded in allowing the viewer to *see* what St. Cecily can *hear* — the celestial music of the angels.

The splendid paintings from these years enhanced Raphael's already considerable reputation, and his fame started to spread throughout Europe.

A New Pope and New Commissions

After the death of Julius II in 1513, Leo X, a man of great learning, assumed the papacy. Raphael was quickly able to interpret the new direction in the visual arts. Little more than thirty years old, he became a leading figure of cultural life in Rome, and was welcomed into the company of scholars and humanists alike. He received an enormous number of appointments and commissions, not only in painting but also in the fields of architecture and archeology, and he was forced to expand his studio and greatly rely upon such assistants as Giulio Romano, Perin del Vaga and Giovanni da Udine.

Leo X shared the ambition of Julius II to restore the power and splendor of ancient times to papal Rome, but he abandoned Julius's policy of enlarging the territories of the church by means of military campaigns, bestowing upon himself the title of "Defender of the Peace."

As was the case with his predecessor, the most eloquent image of Leo X is his portrait by Raphael, which shows Leo seated at a writing desk between two cardinals, Giulio de' Medici (later Pope Clement VII) and Luigi de' Rossi, both of whom were his relatives. Leo's hedonism, humanism and great dignity are captured in the fine rendering of the decorated Bible and the lavishly worked bell that rest on the red velvet of the desk. Leo

24

*The Madonna
of the Diadem*
(detail)

*Portrait of
Joanna of Aragon*

was an art connoisseur and built up a remarkable collection of pictures; he is shown examining the Bible closely with a magnifying glass. The arrangement of the figures and the play of glances between the characters reveal the position of the viewer to be just to the right of the group.

Raphael was also commissioned to paint two other rooms in the Vatican. Given his many other commitments, the greater part of this task was performed by his assistants. One of these rooms, the Sala di Costantino, was completed only after his death. The frescoes in the other room, the Stanza dell'Incendio, finished in 1517, illustrate episodes from the reign of two namesakes of Leo X, Leo II (*The Coronation of Charlemagne* and *The Enthronement of the Pope*) and Leo IV (*The Fire in the Borgo* and *Battle of Ostia*). In the fresco after which this room was named, Raphael showed the miracle of Leo IV, who in 847 is said to have extinguished a dangerous fire that was threatening the Roman quarter of Borgo by making the sign of the cross from a window of the Vatican.

Bramante died soon after the frescoes in the Stanza dell'Incendio were started, and in August 1514 Raphael was nominated his successor and placed in charge of the extensions to St. Peter's Basilica. At the end of the same year he was also asked to make cartoons for ten tapestries to be hung in the Sistine Chapel, which was being used for services while building work was going on in St. Peter's. The ceiling of the chapel had already been painted by Michelangelo, and Leo X intended to complete its decoration with these tapestries.

When preparing the cartoons for the tapestries, Raphael was forced to take several things into account. Given the weaving technique to be used, the whole scene had to be reversed as a mirror image of the final product. The tapestry weavers had a more limited choice of colors, so Raphael painted the cartoons in tempera and used more light and shade to model the figures and backgrounds. The part of the operation over which he had no control was the final weaving, which was done in Brussels. The weavers changed many parts of the original designs, simplifying the figures and landscapes and adding gold and other decorations. The subjects shown in the tapestries were taken from the Acts of the Apostles and were clearly intended to present the reigning pope as the legitimate successor to the first two Apostles of the Church, Peter and Paul, and, paradoxically, as the restorer of its unity.

ARCHITECT AND ARCHEOLOGIST

By the time Raphael was put in charge of the new St. Peter's, he had already acquired a considerable understanding of Renaissance architecture, as can be seen from the temple in *The Marriage of the Virgin* and the grandiose constructions of *The School of Athens*, *The Expulsion of Heliodorus* and *The Mass of Bolsena*. Before the death of Julius II, he had even produced designs for a part of Villa Farnesina, for a funeral chapel for the Chigi family in the Church of Santa Maria del Popolo, and for the Church of Sant'Eligio degli Orefici, all in Rome.

Raphael declared that in his work on St. Peter's his intention was to rediscover the "handsome forms of the ancient buildings." Several projects modifying Bramante's original design to a greater or lesser degree were elaborated before Raphael returned to his earlier idea of grafting a lengthways addition onto the centrally planned construction that his predecessor had started.

In the same period Raphael was busy with other architectural projects, such as the Palazzo Branconio and the palace that he designed for the pope's personal physician, Jacopo da Brescia, where traces of Bramante's influence are interwoven with reinterpreted classical themes.

The most imposing architectural complex ever conceived by Raphael was Villa Madama, commissioned by Leo X and Cardinal Giulio de' Medici. Raphael started work on the villa in 1518, but it was never finished. The structure of the villa, situated on the slopes of Mount Mario, reiterated the forms of the *thermae*, the enormous buildings used by the Romans to house their public baths, and Raphael compensated for the differing levels of the hillside by providing sturdily vaulted rooms; these support the only completed part of the villa, which is richly decorated with reliefs and painted grotesques. In line with his constant attempts to integrate buildings with their natural settings, Raphael also planned a series of gardens and terraces.

Portrait of a Woman
("La Fornarina")

29

Appointed Superintendent of Roman Antiquities in 1515 by Leo X, Raphael was entrusted with the conservation of the city's ruins. Two years later he was ordered to draw up a map of Rome as it had been in the Imperial Age. Raphael set to work on this arduous task helped by a large team of assistants, but the map was not published until 1527, seven years after his death.

Raphael was a great admirer of classical architecture, and it inspired many of his later projects for buildings and paintings. Nevertheless, traces of this interest can be noted in earlier works, particularly in *The Triumph of Galatea*, a fresco painted in 1511 in the Eastern Loggia of Villa Farnesina. The composition is dominated by the female figure at the center, as in Leonardo's *Leda*. The scene maintains its central focus despite the outwards movement of the dolphins guided by the putto in the foreground, recalling another work by Leonardo, *Neptune*. Most striking, however, are such classical elements as the apparent solidity of the surface of the water and the stylized flow of the draperies and of the windswept hair.

A FINAL MASTERPIECE

In 1516 Cardinal Giulio de' Medici commissioned two large altar paintings for the Cathedral of Narbonne, where he was archbishop. *The Transfiguration* was entrusted to Raphael, while *The Raising of Lazarus* was offered to his rival, Sebastiano del Piombo.

Raphael's painting shows two episodes from the Bible, the Transfiguration of Christ on Mount Tabor and the driving out of a demon from a possessed boy, depicted as simultaneous events. This dual theme is used to divide the composition into opposing sections. The upper part depicts the return of Christ to His divine form. Wreathed in light, He ascends from the summit of the mountain, watched by Moses and Elijah. The lower section is pervaded by a sense of agitation, intensified by the rigidity of the gestures and the strong contrasts of light and shade. On the right, the possessed boy is brought before the assembled Apostles. The mother of the boy kneels in the foreground, beseeching them to save her son. Two of the Apostles point towards Christ, the only power able to work such a miracle.

The Transfiguration was started in July 1518, and it was nearing completion at the time of Raphael's death two years later on the artist's thirty-seventh birthday, April 6, 1520. At Raphael's funeral, a solemn occasion attended by the entire papal court, the altarpiece was placed at the head of his coffin while the mourners filed past. The painting was finished by Giulio Romano in 1522, and was hung over the altar of the Church of San Pietro in Montorio.

A GENIUS SHROUDED IN MYSTERY

For all his greatness, we know very little about Raphael the man, and can only make a series of conjectures based on the scant documentary evidence available.

Raphael was regarded by his contemporaries as being the embodiment of Renaissance virtues and graces. They described him as being courteous and respectful with everyone he met, whether they were of noble or humble origin. Perhaps he had been schooled in courtly manners and erudite conversation while still at Urbino; these were gifts that would certainly have helped him in his meteoric rise to fame in Rome. At some point he must have acquired a strong sense of ambition, which may be linked to the premature loss of his parents and their strong influence on his early childhood. In a letter written to an uncle in Urbino in 1508, the artist referred to himself as "your Raphael, painter in Florence," and the image springs to mind of a long-lost nephew writing home to proudly inform his relatives of the consolidation of his career. Later, in Rome, his life was dominated by a burning desire to triumph in every field of art and architecture to which he devoted his energies.

Although we have records of at least two houses purchased by Raphael in Rome, we cannot be certain that he ever married. Vasari, whose writings were often gleaned from hearsay, claimed that Raphael eventually accepted the hand of the niece of a powerful cardinal, at the prelate's insistence. The marriage was never consummated, however, perhaps because Raphael himself was rumored to be destined for a cardinalship. This would not have been unthinkable, as the creation of cardinals was occasionally used as a means of raising money or paying the papal debts, and after so much work for Leo X, Raphael was probably owed a considerable sum. However, it would have been the first time that such an appointment had been made to a painter. According to another tradition, Raphael had already had a lover for many years, a certain Margherita Luti, known as "Fornarina" because she was the daughter of a baker. Vasari claimed that the artist's death was the result of a fever contracted after a particularly intense night of "amorous pleasures," while other sources refer merely to "death from an acute and continuous fever."

Another aspect of Raphael's character can be inferred from his declaration that "the task of the painter is not to do things as nature has done them, but as she ought to do them." This might suggest a certain arrogance, but Raphael's own works attest to the validity of his vision.

Perhaps Cardinal Pietro Bembo, a leading Renaissance scholar, had Raphael's declaration in mind when he wrote his epitaph for the artist's tomb at the Pantheon — which, translated from the Latin, reads: "Here lies Raphael: whilst he lived, nature was in fear of being surpassed; now he is dead, she is in fear of dying."

Raphael was already a legend at the moment of his untimely death, and his work has been popular and revered ever since the classical revival of the seventeenth century. Despite his comparatively brief career, he left a vast number of paintings, frescoes, cartoons, sketches, and designs; and prints based on his works circulated throughout Europe. It has been observed that Raphael's ability to assimilate so many artistic sources made him an important model for all subsequent painters. Art historians today emphasize his fundamental role in the complex cultural evolution of Renaissance ideals, successfully integrating Christianity and classicism in a perfect synthesis.

The Trinity with St. Sebastian and St. Roch

The Madonna of the Book (The "Connestabile Madonna")

Madonna and Child ("Madonna del Granduca")

The Madonna and Child with St. John the Baptist and St. Nicholas of Bari ("The Ansidei Madonna")

The Marriage of the Virgin

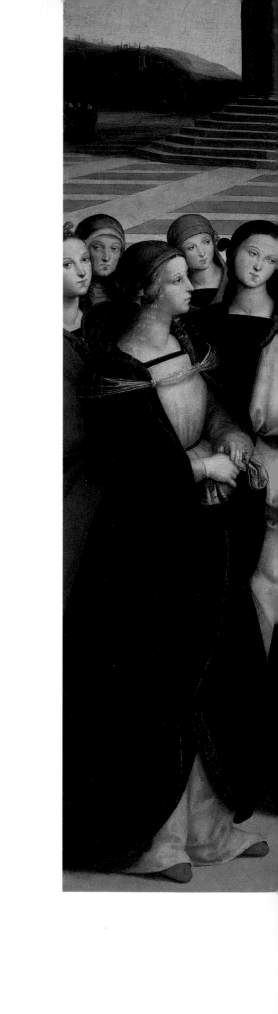

The Marriage of the Virgin (detail)

Self-Portrait

Portrait of a Young Man, probably Francesco Maria della Rovere, Duke of Urbino

St. George and the Dragon

Madonna and Child with Beardless St. Joseph

Portrait of Agnolo Doni

Portrait of Maddalena Doni

The Entombment

The Entombment (detail)

The Madonna and Child with the Infant St. John the Baptist
(*"The Madonna of the Goldfinch"*)

The Madonna and Child with the Infant St. John the Baptist
("La Belle Jardinière")

The Madonna and Child
("The Bridgewater Madonna")

The Holy Family with a Lamb

The Madonna Enthroned with Four Saints
("The Madonna of the Baldacchino")

The Madonna and Child with the Infant St. John the Baptist
("The Esterhezy Madonna")

The Madonna and Child with the Infant St. John the Baptist
("The Aldobrandini Madonna")

The School of Athens

The School of Athens (detail)

The Disputation over the Sacrament ("The Disputa")

Parnassus

Wall of the Stanza della Segnatura illustrating Jurisprudence:
(above) *The Three Cardinal Virtues: Fortitude, Prudence and Temperance;* (left) *Tribonianus Presenting the Pandects to the Emperor Justinian;* (right) *Pope Gregory IX Approving the Decretals*

The Mass of Bolsena

The Expulsion of Heliodorus from the Temple (detail)

The Liberation of St. Peter

Pope Leo I Repulsing Attila

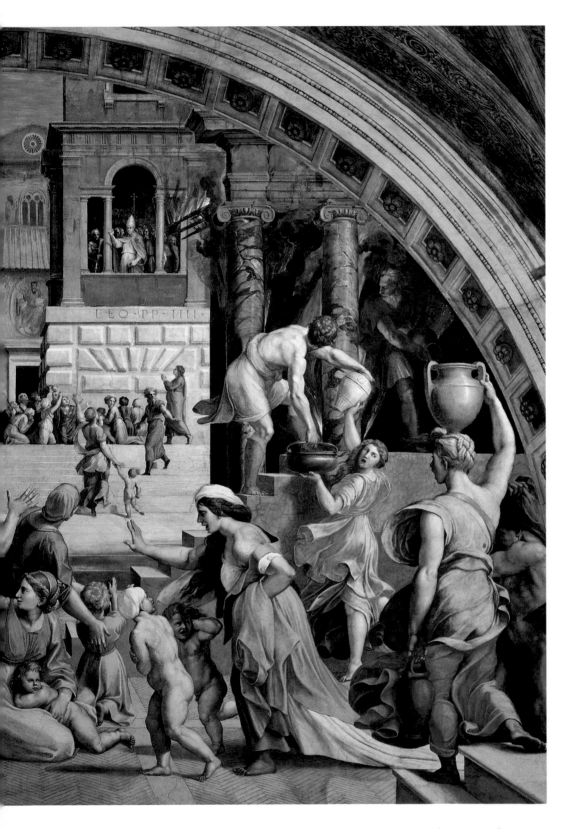

The Fire in the Borgo

The Coronation of Charlemagne

The Triumph of Galatea

The Madonna of the Chair ("Madonna della Sedia")

Portrait of Baldassare Castiglione

Portrait of a Lady with a Veil ("La Velata")

The Sistine Madonna

The Sistine Madonna (detail)

The Miraculous Draft of Fishes

The Holy Family ("Madonna of Francis I")

The Holy Family with the Infant St. John the Baptist
("The Madonna of the Rose")

St. Michael and the Devil

Pope Leo X with Cardinals Giulio de' Medici and Luigi de' Rossi

Pope Leo X with Cardinals Giulio de' Medici and Luigi de' Rossi (detail)

God Creating Animals

The Transfiguration